IN THE LIGHT OF A CHILD

CHRISTMAS

IN THE LIGHT OF A CHILD

A JOURNEY THROUGH THE 52 WEEKS OF THE YEAR
IN BOTH HEMISPHERES
FOR CHILDREN
AND FOR THE CHILD IN EACH HUMAN BEING

MICHAEL HEDLEY BURTON

 ANTHROPOSOPHIC PRESS

Published by Anthroposophic Press
www.anthropress.org

Library of Congress Cataloging-in-Publication Data

Burton, Michael Hedley.
In the light of a child : a journey through the 52 weeks of the year in both hemispheres
for children and for the child in each human being / Michael Hedley Burton.
p. cm.
Summary: A collection of fifty-two verses that examine the course of the year in nature,
arranged so that they can be followed in both northern and southern hemispheres.
ISBN 0-88010-450-3 (paper)
1. Children's poetry, American.
[1. Seasons—Poetry. 2. Nature—Poetry. 3. American poetry.] I. Title.
PS3552.U777I55 1998
811'.54—dc21   97-32633
                                                             CIP
                                                             AC

Cover: Figure by David Gerard; adaptation and lettering by Kitsey McHenry

Frontispiece: R. van der Linden

10 9 8 7 6 5 4

Printed in the United States of America

INTRODUCTORY WORDS

I met a child who stopped me with a glance
and, reading from my darkened eye in disbelief and fear,
said, "Why have you forgotten how to dance?
The Universe is sounding. Only be awake, alive, and hear. . . ."

CHILDREN live deeply into the experience of the seasons. Our own memories bear witness to this — smells, sights, tastes, and feelings which are still strong in us when we recall them later; memories that show how involved and connected with the changing conditions of life around us we then were.

This "at-oneness" with Nature is at first unreflective, unselfconscious and uncritical. But for every child, by a process of inner necessity, there is the gradual fading of the "Garden of Eden" consciousness. Something comes between Nature and the soul, and the child becomes aware of himself as a unique individual whose inner life confronts another world "outside."

This situation can mean for many children times of great loneliness. Shadows begin to be cast by a gradual deepening of the process of thinking. This activity, which should one day restore the human being to a conscious, knowing relationship to life, filled everywhere with the presence of God, is experienced at first as something which divides.

We need to help our children build the new bridges that begin to unite them to the world in a more conscious way. These little verses contain thoughts that are still full of the images of childhood. It is my hope that, if brought to children in a regular way (for instance every morning or evening by a sensitive parent or teacher) seeds will be planted in a child's soul that help him to feel how the world of nature will never become alien to him. Similarly, it is hoped that adults likewise will find nourishment in these verses. Every adult must build his own bridges in later life — to Nature, to other people, and to the field of his own work. What once was given fades and dies and must be consciously rebuilt — this is a law that holds good for all normal human development. But the right seeds planted in childhood help a child to know that the two worlds which he experiences, one "inside" that is the world of his own feelings and the other "outside," are connected and related to each other — that experiences of loneliness, loss and doubt, necessary as obstacles in the path of every striving human being, are not ultimate barriers but temporary periods of resistance to be overcome and learned from.

Our children in the future will have much need of inner strength. These verses have been written for children who are coming towards the beginning of the process which begins around the age of eight or nine. How long the verses can be continued depends upon the child and upon the relationship to the verses that child and adult have managed to achieve.

* * *

It is from Rudolf Steiner's *Calendar of the Soul* that I have drawn the thoughts and images that have been the starting-point for every one of my verses. My experiences with this work of his during periods in both hemispheres and also in the tropics (where most of the verses were written) have led me to the belief that *The Calendar of the Soul* is something of significance for all the earth. And so a second intention of mine in the writing of the verses is the hope that they can help to give human beings a more living feeling for this earth as a whole and thus help people to experience more strongly the sense of brotherhood which results from this.

I have chosen to place the opposite verses together so that what is relevant to people in the Northern Hemisphere is above the corresponding verse for the same week in the Southern Hemisphere. To those who read both, a wonderful feeling for the earth as a whole living being can result. A child could say the verse for a friend, a relative or even other children he doesn't know in the opposite hemisphere, and I believe a very real weaving between souls on earth would take place. These "true" human connections between people become ever more important in the face of their caricature in the phenomena which the technological revolution of our time has placed before us. What takes place heart-to-heart between people is what is important, and in this sphere the creative activity of "the Word" reaches across geographical distances whether small or great. A distinction should always be made between what results from this kind of communication and what comes from the exchange of information by technological means.

* * *

The processes of gradual change in Nature are a picture, a "parable" of changes in the soul. At first we merely take from Nature — she is the mother who provides us with all our needs. More and more we are called upon to give something back to her. Human beings have a holy task to heal and fructify the earth. The fifty-two verses attempt to direct the soul to look at the parables of Nature, the processes of continual interplay between her and ourselves. This dialogue is taking place everywhere. Even a child living in a busy city far from unspoiled Nature can be stimulated to become aware of it and to find the secrets of change and transformation in the many phenomena of his own inner and outer life. Children in the tropics may not see snow outside themselves, but they can be directed to pay heed to the very subtle changes taking place around them that are, at that very moment, growing and intensifying into the true wintry phenomena experienced by those in the temperate latitudes.

I was first drawn to attempt the task of writing these verses out of the conviction that such material — neither prayer nor meditation, but language drawn from Nature herself — was being called for from where there are parents whose children are growing up and preparing for the tasks of their own adult life. Something is needed for these parents and their children that is an outcome of an entirely new striving of humanity directed towards Nature. The children live in a more instinctive relationship to Nature but are moving away from this; the parents have an adult's objectivity but strive to recover, at another level, the vision of childhood and the pure forces of childhood still living within their souls. Thus, adults and children, each with a different way of seeing Nature, and each with a different task to achieve with respect to her, may work together and help one another in a work which has significance for the whole earth.

I have done my best to reflect in the English tongue the wonderful richness and artistry of language present in Rudolf Steiner's verses. I hope that the words which I have written can be brought to life through the spoken word and work into the world as seeds for the future. They are addressed to the Child in each and every one of us, and writing them has truly been for me a labor of love.

— Michael Burton

7

ACKNOWLEDGEMENTS

I would like to thank Percy Compton-Smith and the Taruna Trust who, in large part, have made this publication possible, and Christy Barnes for incredible co-operative labor with me across the oceans in examining and refining the written word. Mei Ling — for whom the first poem (actually verse 52) was written five years ago when she was seven — led me to begin this project, and M.P. it was who kept it in motion.

Most of the verses were written at ''Kahumana'' in Hawaii, and I am indebted to the members of this community who provided me with such a beautiful and creative environment for a year and gave me time to write.

M.H.B.

THE PRAYER OF SAINT BRIDE OF IONA

Christ, King of the Elements, hear me!
    Earth, bear me.
    Water, quicken me.
    Air, lift me.
    Fire, cleanse me.

Christ, King of the Elements, hear me!
    I will bear the burden of earth with thee.
    I will lift my heart to the air to thee.
    I will cleanse my desire for love of thee.
    I will offer my life renewed to thee.

Christ, King of the Elements, hear me!
    Water, fire, air and earth,
    Weave within my heart this day
    A cradle for thy birth.

— Ann Ellerton

9

TO THE READER

Readers in the northern hemisphere should follow, throughout this book, the verses printed in the upper half of these pages, meanwhile glancing down to absorb what their companions on the other side of the earth are experiencing on the very same day as they live in the mood of the opposite season.

Readers in the southern hemisphere should follow the verses they find in the lower half of the page, occasionally looking up to the top of the page to learn what lives in the hearts of those who hear or recite these poems on the other side of the world.

SPRING

1. Northern Hemisphere — Week beginning Easter Sunday.

FROM heaven above comes sunlight streaming;
  Shining, glistening and gleaming.
My silver crescent-cup is filled,
(Be careful that it is not spilled),
Such joy weaves round me everywhere
In water and earth and in light-filled air.
A wave of joy in me as well
Springs from my heart, a surging swell.
By joy I'm taught my God to know.
I am his child — He tells me so.

AUTUMN

27. Southern Hemisphere — Week beginning Easter Sunday.

AND when the golden summer sun grows weaker in our skies,
  I know it really does not die — it just goes through a change.
For it has given its very self to me, in me it lies
    As seed within my deepest heart — a thing most rich and strange.

This sun-seed — I must guard it, precious in my heart as gold.
It will live on in me through nights of winter, dark and cold,
Till lo, in spring a radiant, beauteous flower shall unfold!

2. Northern Hemisphere   — Second week after Easter or Second April week.

ANGELS down to me are bending;
　　Always with me, they are ever caring, tending,
And around me, woven out of love, their flowing mantle they are lending.

I am their child. From out their house of light my soul has wended.
Born of the sun, my seed upon the earth descended.
Good fruit it must bring forth before my life is ended.

28. Southern Hemisphere   — Second week after Easter or Second April week.

REFRESHED, renewed, replenished I am standing
　　Within this world of golden autumn light.
A wondrous, mighty sword the gods are handing
　　To those whose souls with fire of love burn bright.

This flashing sword like sunrays streaming, searing,
　　In darkness shines and makes me firm and sure.
No dragon on my path need I be fearing;
　　I'm armed with light — God-given, sun-forged, pure!

12

3. Northern Hemisphere   — Third week after Easter or Third April week.

THERE once on earth was a Golden Age
    When the veilings of light were a heavenly sign.
When the secrets of Nature were read like a page
    By the people, still wrapped in stars' shimmer and shine.

It's seldom amongst us that gods can be seen;
    And now there are fewer folks friends to the elves.
And yet in this surging of growth and of green,
    My Angel speaks out to the great stars themselves:

"This child that I guide on the world's winding ways,
    He once saw your flame and he knows how it burns.
In the darkness I'll lead him, through life's earthly maze
    Till he win his own strength, and the victory earns."

29. Southern Hemisphere   — Third week after Easter or Third April week.

MY spark of light — it must become a flame.
    Breathe on me, breath of God, it is my aim
    To calmly tend this light within and make it burn up brightly.

The air that nourishes my tender glow —
It's Love! It quickens me. My light shall grow.
    I'm given strength to love all people and to do things rightly.

4. Northern Hemisphere　　　　　— Fourth week after Easter or Fourth April week.

IN spring's sunlit hour
My heart like a flower
Unfolds with great power.

And out into the joyful world
My feeling-forces are unfurled.

All things I love — fire, water, air,
The stones, the stars, the mighty sun,
Plants, creatures, people everywhere
For God is in them, every one.

30. Southern Hemisphere　　　　　— Fourth week after Easter or Fourth April week.

NOW Autumn, like a lusty king,
Strides through the fields — awake, aware.
From summer sleep we've watched him bring
This crispy coolness to the air.

And fruit, well-ripened on the tree,
To me it whispers, round and sweet:
"Be firm. Be strong. Then it shall be
That you'll bear fruit for gods to eat!"

5. Northern Hemisphere   — Fifth week after Easter or First May week.

THE light that is streaming through air all around,
Which, sparkling and gleaming, now warms the earth's ground,
Reveals the stars' handwork where flowers abound.

And, wondrous and radiant, an Angel I see.
He shines with God's light and he smiles upon me.
It is I! He it is whom I one day will be,
In my heavenly mantle, from darkness set free!

31. Southern Hemisphere   — Fifth week after Easter or First May week.

THE light that burns within me — hidden, silent, deep,
It streams with power like the sun from realms of sleep.
It fills my heart with joy. It gives me strength and gladness
And lets me shine to others too, to heal their sadness.

When fire burns and I am master of this fire,
Then, pouring light upon me, Heaven's Sons inspire
My work, and I can do God's deeds as they require.

6. Northern Hemisphere — Sixth week after Easter or Second May week.

ARIS'N in full splendour
  In power and might,
My Angel is speaking
  In weaving of light:

"Remember your homeland.
  From heaven you came.
To lose its remembrance
  Would make you feel shame.

"In light you were living
  Before your life's birth.
Now take of the gifts
  From this garden, the earth.

"Each day growing stronger,
  Let Love be your guide.
Your body the Temple
  Where God may abide."

32. Southern Hemisphere — Sixth week after Easter or Second May week.

MY will is filled with fire and might;
  As days grow shorter, it burns bright!
  I face the world; I have no fear.
  And many things become more clear.
For though there's much that I don't understand as yet,
  I seek for light.

7. Northern Hemisphere   — Seventh week after Easter or Third May week.

DRAWN out into the sheen, the shine, the glisten and the gleam,
    It would be easy to be lost into a dream.

So I must rouse myself and start
To conjure forces of the heart,
Which live within me truly and will bring
The strength and majesty that make me like a king!

Amidst the glory of the sense-world, everywhere displayed,
In sunlit grove and glen and leafy glade,
It is the human heart that rules and reigns supreme!

33. Southern Hemisphere   — Seventh week after Easter or Third May week.

THE world I see:
    A frozen, empty, barren wasteland it would be
        Without the work my head and heart and hands can do
            To heal its pain.

    All things must die and then be born anew.
            To help in this great task, that life be not in vain,
The world needs me.

8. Northern Hemisphere   — Eighth week after Easter or Fourth May week.

LIKE swelling waves that flood the land,
 A green spring-tide is surging, streaming.
Saps flow, touched by a mighty hand
 Whose force we feel, though dimly dreaming.

God weaves amidst the radiant light.
 His helpers work in joyful bliss.
With his creating we unite
 When we, with open hearts, behold all this.

34. Southern Hemisphere   — Eighth week after Easter or Fourth May week.

RICH treasures planted long ago
 Within my soul, so dark and deep,
 Are wakened by my will from sleep.

They stream into the world; they grow.
 They bear star-substances of greatest worth,
 Through loving deeds of mine, uniting heaven and earth.

9. Northern Hemisphere   — Ninth week after Easter or First June week.

THE waves of warmth
    That strongly through the land are radiating, spreading,
Proclaim that we
    To glorious, golden days of summer-sun are heading.

"Be filled with light!"
    My spirit understands these words which Nature everywhere is showing.
"Let thoughts take flight!"
    My heart is told; "Be never earthbound but be always changing, growing!"

35. Southern Hemisphere   — Ninth week after Easter or First June week.

UNTO myself I must be true
    And when my tasks I rightly do,
    Then God, from my own will, the world with light is filling.

Though sometimes I feel weak and small,
I'm linked with love unto the All.
    And I grow stronger when to do God's work I'm willing.

10. Northern Hemisphere — Tenth week after Easter or Second June week.

IN shining majesty the mighty sun,
  A king upon his chariot of gold,
Climbs higher till the heights of heaven are won
  In glory streaming, blesséd to behold.

And watching him, I feel a strange sense grow
  That speaks of things that now I cannot see;
For only later will I truly know
  How at his hour, God's Spirit of the Sun is touching me.

36. Southern Hemisphere — Tenth week after Easter or Second June week.

FROM the deepest part of my heart, I hear
  The voice that must be heard,
  The mighty-sounding Word:

"Let light within you, bright and clear,
  In thoughts and actions, shine.
  Then will you truly be a child of mine."

20

SUMMER

11. Northern Hemisphere   — Eleventh week after Easter or Third June week.

WHEN I look out into the world, I see
   Such wondrous beauty bursting forth in each direction.
When in my heart I look, I feel in me
   How Nature's beauty here must find its true reflection.

For when my heart expands and grows aright,
   When, on the wings of beauty, to the farthest realms of space
                           I'm taken,
Then is my own self lost within the light,
   In quiet joy at last within the arms of God to waken.

WINTER

37. Southern Hemisphere   — Eleventh week after Easter or Third June week.

WITHIN the darkness of the night
   I long to be a light,
That seeds be planted, small but glowing,
Seeds of brightness which start growing....

Soon, in darkness round me, empty, void of light,
God's Word resounds, and all things sparkle pure
                  and clear and bright.

THE light-filled beauty all around me everywhere,
    It calls to me to leave my earthly dwelling,
On wings of fancy sweeping, swooping, soaring light as air,
    Where sun-rays glimmer and where waves of warmth are welling.

My Angel calls — his love I shall not shun;
For in the sparkling light and glowing warmth of sun,
With joy we fly together — and are truly one.

A ROSE of pure white blooms in midnight's dark hour.
    The spell of the darkness is broken and torn.
In my heart there's a bursting of magical power
    For the heavenly Child on earth has been born!

He is pure as the snow. With my heart's love aglow
I shall nourish this Child, and he surely shall grow!

13. Northern Hemisphere   — Fifth June week.

AND as I deeply drink
    From all the rich gifts Nature is bestowing,
In me, the longing for a link
With the wise and powerful Sons of Heaven starts flaming, growing.

For rank on rank I see
    Upon a golden stairway, Angels moving in a mighty throng.
They beckon me,
    And I begin to climb, for certainly among their ranks, I too belong.

39. Southern Hemisphere   — Fifth June week.

I LISTEN to all that the Angels are saying.
    They give me their light, spun on threads of pure gold.
They grant me new power in living, in praying.
    They bring me rich gifts which I carefully hold.

The Child at his mother's breast stirs and wakes slowly.
This gold makes a mantle to clothe him most holy.

14. Northern Hemisphere   — First July week.

I HAVE lived with the wind, with the clouds, with the showers;
    I have hearkened to speech without words.
I have joyed with the joys of the blossoming flowers,
    And joined the sweet song of the birds.
I have danced to the dance that all Nature is dancing,
The hedgehog so serious, the wild pony prancing;
Ah Life, lovely Life, you are young and entrancing....

But the stars, gleaming down on me, waken me now.
To their strong, silent speech I must listen somehow.

40. Southern Hemisphere   — First July week.

A ND as I live in depths of Mystery so deep,
    I feel how silver waves, which gleam and glisten as they're
        swept and swirled
From my own heart, like lovely lights seen through a veil of sleep,
    Go forth: true love, arising, surging from the darkness out
        into the world.

All vain illusions flee! They must not stay
When my heart's feelings, true and tender as a rose, unfold
        to greet the day.

15. Northern Hemisphere — Second July week.

IN shimmering of dim, enchanted dreaming,
  A shining veil of light enwraps me round.
Behind it Angels work, whose mighty streaming
  Sends strength to me and gives my feet firm ground.

  I love the sun's warm light, so gold and fair.
  I love the sun's bright rays which burst and sparkle everywhere,
As light and shadow weave amidst the forest, greenly gleaming.

41. Southern Hemisphere — Second July week.

THE power of my heart's bright flame
  Is striving to stream out through cold and dark.
God gives me power to fulfill my aim,
  That fires of love be kindled from each golden spark.

A heart of love that in the dark is brightly burning
Will mean that often to do deeds of love my hands are turning.

NOW must I build a worthy place
    Wherein the Sun may shine aright.
My arms enfold him — gift of grace,
    Born of the sheen of summer's light.

To form this house takes care and skill and art;
Where is this Sun? It dwells within my heart.

WHEN winter wraps a mantle dark and drear
    Around the world beyond my own warm hearth,
Then am I called to rise and conquer fear
    And bravely meet this darkness in my path.

My light each day in brightness is increasing.
    Its glow of warmth reveals the stir of life.
The light-stream of my heart is never-ceasing.
    And so I'm strong, come grief or pain or strife.

17. Northern Hemisphere   — Fourth July week.

THE sun, which gleams and streams over land and sea,
    Shines also from my eyes, for it has entered me.

It speaks of what I still must do.
I hear it as a Word most true:

"Oh, your heart must be great, must be wide, must be bold,
All things your soul must gather and hold,
This whole wonderful world with your love to enfold."

43. Southern Hemisphere   — Fourth July week.

IN wintry depths of night
    The majesty of heaven is so close to me,
Because my heart's new power and might
    Makes real and full of substance all the things I see.

There flames in me, against all ice and frost, all rain and sleet,
The leaping, dancing fire-forces of my heart to give me
                    light and heat.

18.   Northern Hemisphere — Fifth July week.

WITHIN my heart there lives the sun;
　　The Child of Love his journey to an earthly dwelling
　　　　has begun.
He will be born on winter's holy night;
But can I now begin to make a place where he can grow aright?
For I must weave a radiant garment, rich and rare,
In which to wrap and hold the wondrous Child so fair.

44.   Southern Hemisphere — Fifth July week.

IT'S wintry still, but out of death — new birth!
　　This is life's law, and now I should look well
For signs that spring will come onto the earth,
　　For she prepares, and soon her power will swell:

New shoots prepare to sprout on many a tree.
A new note in the birdsong... and more clues as well I see...

But midst this change, I must be true;
Be firm and strong in all I do.

19. Northern Hemisphere

— First August week.

DEAR Child of Light, all that you've given I won't forget;
    I'll work each day to build for you a special place
And in my heart prepare a sacred space.

    My striving sometimes fails — and yet
        I grow a little every day,
        And journey further on my way.

45. Southern Hemisphere

— First August week.

MY firmness and strength gives me ground that is sure,
    For the light of the Child is gentle and pure.
All things become bathed with his healing, gold light
When I look at the world with his love in my sight.

Watch the gnomes split and crumble the stuff of the earth,
While the light, airy sylphs bring a green world to birth.

With great joy I am learning to give what they need,
For I bring them the light, and they're grateful indeed!

20. Northern Hemisphere — Second August week.

MYSELF in my aloneness I must feel.
　　What if I did not love? Then would there be
　　　No bridge to others. I would live in fear.

　　Love leads me out to flower, star and tree,
　　　　To rushing river and to people dear;
　If I am lonely, only love has power to heal.

46. Southern Hemisphere — Second August week.

MY light is pressed by darkness round;
　　It is not easy to stay upright, strong and sound!
The Dragon, lurking, would devour
My shining radiance with his power.

But I, remembering how on winter's Holy Night,
In darkness shone the Midnight Sun that is the world's true Light,
Need have no fear of dragons wild
For I am led by the Holy Child.

21. Northern Hemisphere   — Third August week.

SOMETHING new is mounting, growing
    Deep within me, outward surging.
Seed is ripening, sap is flowing;
    Power streaming, light emerging.

Fire-spirits sparkle round me, warmth and will-bestowing:
    "Sing our fiery song of summer strength!" I hear them urging.

47. Southern Hemisphere   — Third August week.

NOW springing from the fertile Mother of all living things,
    the Earth,
Comes joy-of-growth, as power leading all her children unto birth.
    My life is charmed, my strength is sure,
    For I am armed — my heart is pure;
And I can join amidst this joy and merriment with radiant mirth!

THE light rains down. My king, in this late-summer hour,
  You reign within my heart as well, with growing power.
You shine with strength. You gleam and glance and glisten.
You lead me into depths where I, within the silence, learn to listen.

And there you form life's fruits, fruits good to eat,
In weaving soul-light warm, where they grow ripe and rich and sweet.

BRIGHT the sun's gold rays are streaming;
  Streaming fills my soul with light.
Light becomes a sword of radiance,
  Radiance flashing in dark night.
Night is banished. See Love's sun-rise,
  Love's Sun rising, warm and bright.

23. Northern Hemisphere   — First September week.

IN misty, moisty autumn air,
    Summer lingers still through mellow days,
And light which glimmers gold and fair
    Is dimmed and dulled by gentle veils of haze.

I myself can clearly see
    How autumn, soft and slow, is creeping.
Summer gave herself to me
    And now departs for winter-sleeping.

49. Southern Hemisphere   — First September week.

THE silent strength of starlight's gleam
    Is filling my soul with new heavenly might.
In darkness of winter, I woke from a dream
    Like a child from sleep in the middle of night.
Now new hope is dawning — strong and supreme,
    And declaring, "Go forth out of darkness to light!"

IN striving forth toward the goal,
I feel new firmness in my soul.
The I-of-God in knowing sight
Fills all my will with gleaming light.

And in these hidden depths, this radiant glow,
By bringing light to darkness, makes the good fruit grow.

50. Southern Hemisphere — Second September week.

SPIRITS of water, spirits of air,
Weave in the world full of nurture and care.
Sons of bright fire and gnomes of quick gait —
All of them speak to me whilst they create:

"Oh, we work within the world for purest joyfulness alone,
But remember please the deeds we do — they must not
pass unknown,
For you free us from enchantment when you make
our life your own."

25. Northern Hemisphere

THOUGH much is changing, I stand strong
　　And in the darkness, shine.
For sleep, the plants and creatures long
　　But I have work divine.

For sun-seeds golden I'll be sowing,
Warmly from my heart's depth's glowing,
　　Into winter's icy flowing.

51. Southern Hemisphere

THE beauty of all things, radiant and fair,
　　How it pours through my heart; how it fills me with gladness!
In the people I meet this same beauty is there;
　　It reflects in their eyes, both in joy and in sadness.

And when our eyes sparkle or twinkle or shine,
　　When warm love is flowing in the way that we live,
Then the water of life in ourselves becomes wine,
　　And to God this can be the great gift that we give.

26.   Northern Hemisphere   — Michaelmas; Fourth September week.

O Nature, you are as a mother to me,
    Giving me strength and nourishing me.
I feel you near me and nearer still.
You fill me with fire — how strong is my will!
To be doing what's good is what I desire,
And I shall, for I'm filled with God's heavenly fire.

52.   Southern Hemisphere   — Michaelmas; Fourth September week.

F ROM deep in my heart this world I love —
    The green, green hills and the mountains above,
The sea so blue and the sunlight gold,
And everything that I behold.

And I become stronger as I grow,
For all of God's Angels are with me I know.
Angels of water, fire, earth and air,
Always stay by me. This is my prayer.

AUTUMN

27. Northern Hemisphere — First October week.

AND when the golden summer sun grows weaker in our skies,
I know it really does not die — it just goes through a change.
For it has given its very self to me, in me it lies
As seed within my deepest heart — a thing most rich and strange.

This sun-seed — I must guard it, precious in my heart as gold.
It will live on in me through nights of winter, dark and cold,
Till lo, in spring a radiant, beauteous flower shall unfold!

SPRING

1. Southern Hemisphere — First October week.

FROM heaven above comes sunlight streaming;
Shining, glistening and gleaming.
My silver crescent-cup is filled,
(Be careful that it is not spilled),
Such joy weaves round me everywhere
In water and earth and in light-filled air.
A wave of joy in me as well
Springs from my heart, a surging swell.
By joy I'm taught my God to know.
I am his child — He tells me so.

28. Northern Hemisphere   — Second October week.

REFRESHED, renewed, replenished I am standing
     Within this world of golden autumn light.
A wondrous, mighty sword the gods are handing
     To those whose souls with fire of love burn bright.

This flashing sword like sunrays streaming, searing,
     In darkness shines and makes me firm and sure.
No dragon on my path need I be fearing;
     I'm armed with light — God-given, sun-forged, pure!

2. Southern Hemisphere   — Second October week.

ANGELS down to me are bending;
     Always with me, they are ever caring, tending,
And around me, woven out of love, their flowing mantle they are lending.

I am their child. From out their house of light my soul has wended.
Born of the sun, my seed upon the earth descended.
Good fruit it must bring forth before my life is ended.

29. Northern Hemisphere   — Third October week.

MY spark of light — it must become a flame.
    Breathe on me, breath of God, it is my aim
To calmly tend this light within and make it burn up brightly.

The air that nourishes my tender glow —
It's Love! It quickens me. My light shall grow.
    I'm given strength to love all people and to do things rightly.

3. Southern Hemisphere   — Third October week.

THERE once on earth was a Golden Age
    When the veilings of light were a heavenly sign.
When the secrets of Nature were read like a page
    By the people, still wrapped in stars' shimmer and shine.

It's seldom amongst us that gods can be seen;
    And now there are fewer folks friends to the elves.
And yet in this surging of growth and of green,
    My Angel speaks out to the great stars themselves:

"This child that I guide on the world's winding ways,
    He once saw your flame and he knows how it burns.
In the darkness I'll lead him, through life's earthly maze
    Till he win his own strength, and the victory earns."

NOW Autumn, like a lusty king,
  Strides through the fields — awake, aware.
From summer sleep we've watched him bring
  This crispy coolness to the air.

And fruit, well-ripened on the tree,
  To me it whispers, round and sweet:
"Be firm. Be strong. Then it shall be
  That you'll bear fruit for gods to eat!"

4. Southern Hemisphere — Fourth October week.

IN spring's sunlit hour
  My heart like a flower
Unfolds with great power.

And out into the joyful world
My feeling-forces are unfurled.

All things I love — fire, water, air,
  The stones, the stars, the mighty sun,
Plants, creatures, people everywhere
  For God is in them, every one.

31. Northern Hemisphere   — First November week.

THE light that burns within me — hidden, silent, deep,
It streams with power like the sun from realms of sleep.
It fills my heart with joy. It gives me strength and gladness
And lets me shine to others too, to heal their sadness.

When fire burns and I am master of this fire,
Then, pouring light upon me, Heaven's Sons inspire
My work, and I can do God's deeds as they require.

5. Southern Hemisphere   — First November week.

THE light that is streaming through air all around,
Which, sparkling and gleaming, now warms the earth's ground,
Reveals the stars' handwork where flowers abound.

And, wondrous and radiant, an Angel I see.
He shines with God's light and he smiles upon me.
It is I! He it is whom I one day will be,
In my heavenly mantle, from darkness set free!

41

MY will is filled with fire and might;
As days grow shorter, it burns bright!
I face the world; I have no fear.
And many things become more clear.
For though there's much that I don't understand as yet,
I seek for light.

6. Southern Hemisphere — Second November week.

ARIS'N in full splendour
In power and might,
My Angel is speaking
In weaving of light:

"Remember your homeland.
From heaven you came.
To lose its remembrance
Would make you feel shame.

"In light you were living
Before your life's birth.
Now take of the gifts
From this garden, the earth.

"Each day growing stronger,
Let Love be your guide.
Your body the Temple
Where God may abide."

THE world I see:
A frozen, empty, barren wasteland it would be
Without the work my head and heart and hands can do
To heal its pain.

All things must die and then be born anew.
To help in this great task, that life be not in vain,
The world needs me.

DRAWN out into the sheen, the shine, the glisten and the gleam,
It would be easy to be lost into a dream.

So I must rouse myself and start
To conjure forces of the heart,
Which live within me truly and will bring
The strength and majesty that make me like a king!

Amidst the glory of the sense-world, everywhere displayed,
In sunlit grove and glen and leafy glade,
It is the human heart that rules and reigns supreme!

RICH treasures planted long ago
  Within my soul, so dark and deep,
Are wakened by my will from sleep.

They stream into the world; they grow.
  They bear star-substances of greatest worth,
  Through loving deeds of mine, uniting heaven and earth.

8. Southern Hemisphere — Fourth November week.

LIKE swelling waves that flood the land,
  A green spring-tide is surging, streaming.
Saps flow, touched by a mighty hand
  Whose force we feel, though dimly dreaming.

God weaves amidst the radiant light.
  His helpers work in joyful bliss.
With his creating we unite
  When we, with open hearts, behold all this.

35. Northern Hemisphere — First December week.

UNTO myself I must be true
  And when my tasks I rightly do,
Then God, from my own will, the world with light is filling.

Though sometimes I feel weak and small,
I'm linked with love unto the All.
  And I grow stronger when to do God's work I'm willing.

9. Southern Hemisphere — First December week.

THE waves of warmth
  That strongly through the land are radiating, spreading,
Proclaim that we
  To glorious, golden days of summer-sun are heading.

"Be filled with light!"
  My spirit understands these words which Nature everywhere is showing.
"Let thoughts take flight!"
  My heart is told; "Be never earthbound but be always changing, growing!"

FROM the deepest part of my heart, I hear
The voice that must be heard,
The mighty-sounding Word:

"Let light within you, bright and clear,
In thoughts and actions, shine.
Then will you truly be a child of mine."

10.   Southern Hemisphere   — Second December week.

IN shining majesty the mighty sun,
A king upon his chariot of gold,
Climbs higher till the heights of heaven are won
In glory streaming, blessèd to behold.

And watching him, I feel a strange sense grow
That speaks of things that now I cannot see;
For only later will I truly know
How at his hour, God's Spirit of the Sun is touching me.

WINTER

WITHIN the darkness of the night
I long to be a light,
That seeds be planted, small but glowing,
Seeds of brightness which start growing....

Soon, in darkness round me, empty, void of light,
God's Word resounds, and all things sparkle pure
and clear and bright.

SUMMER

WHEN I look out into the world, I see
Such wondrous beauty bursting forth in each direction.
When in my heart I look, I feel in me
How Nature's beauty here must find its true reflection.

For when my heart expands and grows aright,
When, on the wings of beauty, to the farthest realms of space
I'm taken,
Then is my own self lost within the light,
In quiet joy at last within the arms of God to waken.

38. Northern Hemisphere   — Christmas; Fourth December week.

AROSE of pure white blooms in midnight's dark hour.
The spell of the darkness is broken and torn.
In my heart there's a bursting of magical power
For the heavenly Child on earth has been born!

He is pure as the snow. With my heart's love aglow
I shall nourish this Child, and he surely shall grow!

12. Southern Hemisphere   — Christmas; Fourth December week.

THE light-filled beauty all around me everywhere,
It calls to me to leave my earthly dwelling,
On wings of fancy sweeping, swooping, soaring light as air,
Where sun-rays glimmer and where waves of warmth are welling.

My Angel calls — his love I shall not shun;
For in the sparkling light and glowing warmth of sun,
With joy we fly together — and are truly one.

I LISTEN to all that the Angels are saying.
　　They give me their light, spun on threads of pure gold.
They grant me new power in living, in praying.
　　They bring me rich gifts which I carefully hold.

The Child at his mother's breast stirs and wakes slowly.
This gold makes a mantle to clothe him most holy.

AND as I deeply drink
　　From all the rich gifts Nature is bestowing,
In me, the longing for a link
With the wise and powerful Sons of Heaven starts flaming, growing.

For rank on rank I see
　　Upon a golden stairway, Angels moving in a mighty throng.
They beckon me,
　　And I begin to climb, for certainly among their ranks, I too belong.

40. Northern Hemisphere — First January week.

AND as I live in depths of Mystery so deep,
    I feel how silver waves, which gleam and glisten as they're
        swept and swirled
From my own heart, like lovely lights seen through a veil of sleep,
    Go forth: true love, arising, surging from the darkness out
        into the world.

All vain illusions flee! They must not stay
When my heart's feelings, true and tender as a rose, unfold
        to greet the day.

14. Southern Hemisphere — First January week.

I HAVE lived with the wind, with the clouds, with the showers;
    I have hearkened to speech without words.
I have joyed with the joys of the blossoming flowers,
    And joined the sweet song of the birds.
I have danced to the dance that all Nature is dancing,
The hedgehog so serious, the wild pony prancing;
Ah Life, lovely Life, you are young and entrancing....

But the stars, gleaming down on me, waken me now.
To their strong, silent speech I must listen somehow.

41. Northern Hemisphere — Second January week.

THE power of my heart's bright flame
    Is striving to stream out through cold and dark.
God gives me power to fulfill my aim,
    That fires of love be kindled from each golden spark.

A heart of love that in the dark is brightly burning
Will mean that often to do deeds of love my hands are turning.

15. Southern Hemisphere — Second January week.

IN shimmering of dim, enchanted dreaming,
    A shining veil of light enwraps me round.
Behind it Angels work, whose mighty streaming
    Sends strength to me and gives my feet firm ground.

    I love the sun's warm light, so gold and fair.
    I love the sun's bright rays which burst and sparkle everywhere,
As light and shadow weave amidst the forest, greenly gleaming.

WHEN winter wraps a mantle dark and drear
　　　Around the world beyond my own warm hearth,
Then am I called to rise and conquer fear
　　　And bravely meet this darkness in my path.

My light each day in brightness is increasing.
　　　Its glow of warmth reveals the stir of life.
The light-stream of my heart is never-ceasing.
　　　And so I'm strong, come grief or pain or strife.

NOW must I build a worthy place
　　　Wherein the Sun may shine aright.
My arms enfold him — gift of grace,
　　　Born of the sheen of summer's light.

To form this house takes care and skill and art;
Where is this Sun? It dwells within my heart.

43. Northern Hemisphere   — Fourth January week.

IN wintry depths of night
    The majesty of heaven is so close to me,
Because my heart's new power and might
    Makes real and full of substance all the things I see.

There flames in me, against all ice and frost, all rain and sleet,
The leaping, dancing fire-forces of my heart to give me
                light and heat.

17. Southern Hemisphere   — Fourth January week.

THE sun, which gleams and streams over land and sea,
    Shines also from my eyes, for it has entered me.

It speaks of what I still must do.
I hear it as a Word most true:

"Oh, your heart must be great, must be wide, must be bold,
All things your soul must gather and hold,
This whole wonderful world with your love to enfold."

44. Northern Hemisphere — Fifth July week.

IT'S wintry still, but out of death — new birth!
 This is life's law, and now I should look well
For signs that spring will come onto the earth,
 For she prepares, and soon her power will swell:

New shoots sprout green on every tree.
A new note in the birdsong... and more clues as well I see...

But midst this change, I must be true;
Be firm and strong in all I do.

18. Southern Hemisphere — Fifth July week.

WITHIN my heart there lives the sun;
 The Child of Love his journey to an earthly dwelling
 has begun.
He will be born on winter's holy night;
But can I now begin to make a place where he can grow aright?
For I must weave a radiant garment, rich and rare,
In which to wrap and hold the wondrous Child so fair.

MY firmness and strength gives me ground that is sure,
For the light of the Child is gentle and pure.
All things become bathed with his healing, gold light
When I look at the world with his love in my sight.

Watch the gnomes split and crumble the stuff of the earth,
While the light, airy sylphs bring a green world to birth.

With great joy I am learning to give what they need,
For I bring them the light, and they're grateful indeed!

DEAR Child of Light, all that you've given I won't forget;
I'll work each day to build for you a special place
And in my heart prepare a sacred space.

My striving sometimes fails — and yet
I grow a little every day,
And journey further on my way.

46. Northern Hemisphere   — Second February week.

MY light is pressed by darkness round;
 It is not easy to stay upright, strong and sound!
The Dragon, lurking, would devour
My shining radiance with his power.

But I, remembering how on winter's Holy Night,
In darkness shone the Midnight Sun that is the world's true Light,
Need have no fear of dragons wild
For I am led by the Holy Child.

20. Southern Hemisphere   — Second February week.

MYSELF in my aloneness I must feel.
 What if I did not love? Then would there be
 No bridge to others. I would live in fear.

Love leads me out to flower, star and tree,
 To rushing river and to people dear;
If I am lonely, only love has power to heal.

47. Northern Hemisphere   — Third February week.

NOW springing from the fertile Mother of all living things,
      the Earth,
Comes joy-of-growth, as power leading all her children unto birth.
    My life is charmed, my strength is sure,
    For I am armed — my heart is pure;
And I can join amidst this joy and merriment with radiant mirth!

21. Southern Hemisphere   — Third February week.

SOMETHING new is mounting, growing
    Deep within me, outward surging.
Seed is ripening, sap is flowing;
    Power streaming, light emerging.

Fire-spirits sparkle round me, warmth and will-bestowing:
    "Sing our fiery song of summer strength!" I hear them urging.

BRIGHT the sun's gold rays are streaming;
  Streaming fills my soul with light.
Light becomes a sword of radiance,
  Radiance flashing in dark night.
Night is banished. See Love's sun-rise,
  Love's Sun rising, warm and bright.

THE light rains down. My king, in this late-summer hour,
  You reign within my heart as well, with growing power.
You shine with strength. You gleam and glance and glisten.
You lead me into depths where I, within the silence, learn to listen.

And there you form life's fruits, fruits good to eat,
In weaving soul-light warm, where they grow ripe and rich and sweet.

THE silent strength of starlight's gleam
    Is filling my soul with new heavenly might.
In darkness of winter, I woke from a dream
    Like a child from sleep in the middle of night.
Now new hope is dawning — strong and supreme,
    And declaring, "Go forth out of darkness to light!"

23. Southern Hemisphere — First March week.

IN misty, moisty autumn air,
    Summer lingers still through mellow days,
And light which glimmers gold and fair
    Is dimmed and dulled by gentle veils of haze.

I myself can clearly see
    How autumn, soft and slow, is creeping.
Summer gave herself to me
    And now departs for winter-sleeping.

SPIRITS of water, spirits of air,
Weave in the world full of nurture and care.
Sons of bright fire and gnomes of quick gait —
All of them speak to me whilst they create:

"Oh, we work within the world for purest joyfulness alone,
But remember please the deeds we do — they must not
pass unknown,
For you free us from enchantment when you make
our life your own."

24. Southern Hemisphere — Second March week.

IN striving forth toward the goal,
I feel new firmness in my soul.
The I-of-God in knowing sight
Fills all my will with gleaming light.

And in these hidden depths, this radiant glow,
By bringing light to darkness, makes the good fruit grow.

51. Northern Hemisphere   — Third March week.

THE beauty of all things, radiant and fair,
     How it pours through my heart; how it fills me with gladness!
In the people I meet this same beauty is there;
     It reflects in their eyes, both in joy and in sadness.

And when our eyes sparkle or twinkle or shine,
     When warm love is flowing in the way that we live,
Then the water of life in ourselves becomes wine,
     And to God this can be the great gift that we give.

25. Southern Hemisphere   — Third March week.

THOUGH much is changing, I stand strong
     And in the darkness, shine.
For sleep, the plants and creatures long
     But I have work divine.

For sun-seeds golden I'll be sowing,
Warmly from my heart's depth's glowing,
     Into winter's icy flowing.

FROM deep in my heart this world I love —
The green, green hills and the mountains above,
The sea so blue and the sunlight gold,
And everything that I behold.

And I become stronger as I grow,
For all of God's Angels are with me I know.
Angels of water, fire, earth and air,
Always stay by me. This is my prayer.

26. Southern Hemisphere — Fourth March week.

O Nature, you are as a mother to me,
Giving me strength and nourishing me.
I feel you near me and nearer still.
You fill me with fire — how strong is my will!
To be doing what's good is what I desire,
And I shall, for I'm filled with God's heavenly fire.